The Best of The **MAILBOX**

Bears

Our best bear activities and reproducibles from the 2000–2011 issues of *The Mailbox* and *Teacher's Helper* magazines

- **Literacy activities**
- **Learning centers**
- **Group-time activities**
- **Songs**

- **Math activities**
- **Arts-and-crafts ideas**
- **...and more!**

Fun and practical skills practice!

Managing Editor: Brenda Fay

Editorial Team: Becky S. Andrews, Diane Badden, Kimberley Bruck, Karen A. Brudnak, Pam Crane, Chris Curry, David Drews, Tazmen Fisher Hansen, Marsha Heim, Lori Z. Henry, Mark Rainey, Greg D. Rieves, Hope Rodgers-Medina, Rebecca Saunders, Donna K. Teal, Sharon M. Tresino, Zane Williard

www.themailbox.com

Printed in the United States
10 9 8 7 6 5 4 3 2 1

HPS246114

Table of Contents

Thematic Units

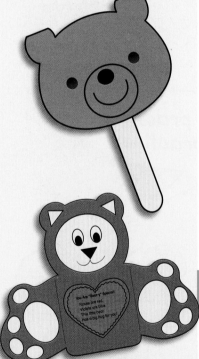

Cuddly and Cute!

Teddy Bear Centers

A "Bear-y" Yummy Snack

Math Center

This adorable activity spotlights counting and presubtraction skills! Provide a stuffed teddy bear, a bowl, pom-poms (berries), and a large die. A child rolls the die, counts the dots aloud, and places that many berries in the bowl. Next, he pretends to feed the bear one berry and then sets that berry aside. He counts the remaining berries to see how many are left; then he continues in the same way until the bowl is empty.

adapted from an idea by Elizabeth Cook, St. Louis, MO

Save the Teddy Bears!

Water Table

Place teddy bear manipulatives in your water table. Gather disposable bowls (rescue boats) that match the colors of the teddy bears; then float the bowls in the water table. Provide slotted spoons. A youngster uses a spoon to pick up each bear and place it in its matching boat. After all the passengers are aboard their appropriate boats, the child gently pushes or blows the boats through the water.

Amber Dingman, Sterling, MI

T Is for Teddy

Literacy Center

Place several stuffed teddy bears and letter *T* cards in your block center. Encourage youngsters to study the letter and then arrange blocks on the floor to make *T*s. Have each student place a teddy bear next to each *T*.

Patches

Art Center

These patched-up teddy bears are simple and sweet! For each child, make a brown construction paper copy of page 5. Provide squares of felt, fabric, scrapbook paper, and tissue paper. A child brushes glue inside the bear outline. Then he presses squares over the glue. When the project is dry, cut out the teddy bear.

Teddy Bear Spa

Dramatic-Play Area

Stock the area with stuffed teddy bears and personal care and spa items, such as a plastic tub, empty body wash bottles, washcloths, towels, receiving blankets (for body wraps), a small table (for massages), hair brushes, and hair accessories. Also provide a toy cash register, play money, a toy phone, an appointment book, and writing tools. A youngster uses the items to engage in pretend spa-related play.

Elizabeth Cook, St. Louis, MO

TEC61387

Math With Goldilocks and the Three Bears

Three bears, three bowls, three beds, and three chairs—*Goldilocks and the Three Bears* is a tale just meant to encourage math skills!

Are There Three?

Counting

The three bears have three of everything! With this activity, youngsters decide if sets of items belong to the three bears. In advance, gather sets of household items, such as five cups, three toothbrushes, four towels, two shampoo bottles, three pillows, and three combs. Remind youngsters that the three bears had three bowls, three beds, and three chairs. Then present one set of items. Lead youngsters in counting the set. Then ask if the items belong to the three bears, helping students conclude that the items can only belong to the bears if there are three. Continue in the same way with each set of items.

Cindy Barber, Fredonia, WI

So Much Porridge!

Exploring volume

Place uncooked oatmeal (porridge) in your sensory table and provide a cooking pot, measuring cups and spoons, and plastic bowls in three different sizes. Youngsters use the measuring cups and spoons to scoop and pour the porridge into the bowls.

Janet Boyce, Cokato, MN

Small, Medium, Large

Ordering by size

Cut out a copy of the bear patterns on page 8. Also make bowl, chair, and bed cutouts in three different sizes (see pages 9 and 10 for patterns). Attach a piece of felt to the back of each cutout to ready it for flannelboard use. Next, help students arrange the bears, bowls, chairs, and beds on your flannelboard in rows ordered from smallest to largest. Then help students point to the cutouts to retell the story.

Golden Curls

Comparing length

Cut and curl lengths of yellow curling ribbon (curls), making some pieces long and others short. Place the curls in a tub. Then place the tub at a center along with containers labeled as shown. A youngster chooses a curl and decides whether it is long or short. Then she places it in the correct container. If desired, when each youngster has had a chance to visit the center, place the curls back in the tub along with pairs of scissors. Then encourage youngsters to exercise fine-motor skills by snipping Goldilocks's curls.

Janet Boyce, Cokato, MN

long

short

Tasty or Not?

Organizing data

Place two plastic hoops on the floor and label one hoop with the words "I like it" and the second hoop with the words "I don't like it." To begin, help each youngster pour a packet of instant oatmeal (porridge) into a disposable bowl. Then help him stir warm water into the porridge. After he eats his porridge, have him place a bear counter in the appropriate hoop to show whether he likes or dislikes the porridge. Lead students in counting and comparing the number of bears in the hoops.

Carole Watkins, Holy Family Child Care Center, Crown Point, IN
Linda Tharp, Hickory Child Development Center, Bel Air, MD

Bear Patterns

Use with "Small, Medium, Large" on page 7.

TEC61387

TEC61387

TEC61387

Bed Pattern
Use with "Small, Medium, Large" on page 7.

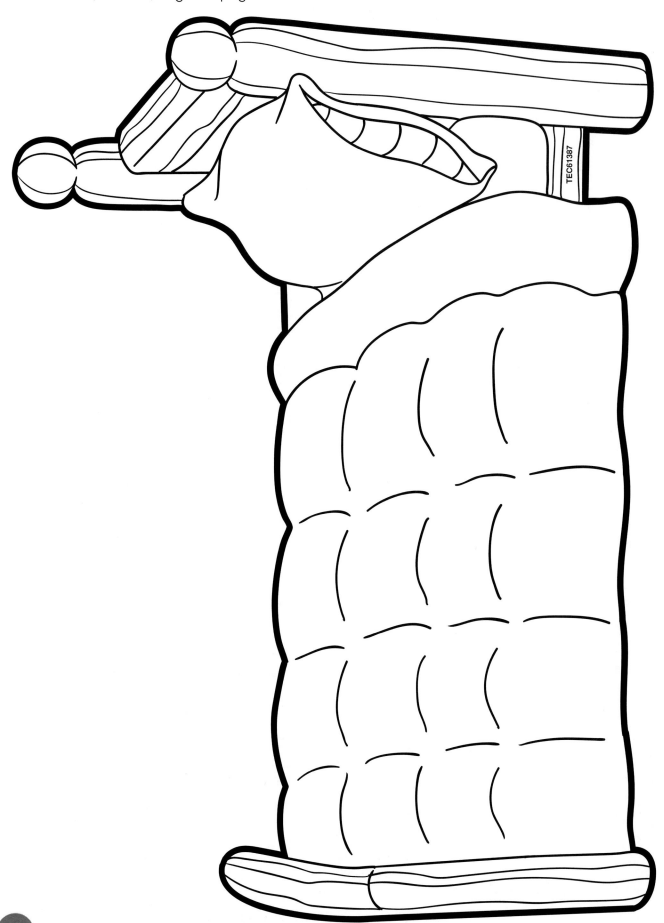

TEC61387

Beginning Letter Bears

What happens when *A* is paired with Astronaut Bear and *M* is paired with Magician Bear? Students make memorable letter-sound connections!

idea by Terri Strong, Santa Paula, CA

A Booklet of Bears

Give students' beginning sound skills a boost with this booklet project. Have students contribute pages to make a class booklet or make booklets of their own using the directions below. Alphabetize the completed pages, place a cover on top, and then bind the project as desired.

To make a booklet page:
1. Cut out a brown construction paper copy of the bear pattern on page 13.
2. Glue the cutout on a sheet of construction paper.
3. Label the top right corner with a letter.
4. Choose a job that begins with the corresponding letter's sound.
5. Use paper scraps and craft supplies to decorate the bear to match its job.

Possible Bear Jobs

actor, astronaut	jeweler, judge	sailor, singer
baker, ballerina	key maker, king	teacher, tennis player
carpenter, conductor	librarian, lifeguard	umpire, usher
dentist, doctor	magician, mail carrier	violinist, veterinarian
electrician, engineer	newscaster, nurse	waiter, waitress
farmer, firefighter	oceanographer, office worker	X-ray technician
goalie, guitarist	poet, police officer	yard worker, yarn maker
hairstylist, housekeeper	queen, quilter	zookeeper, zoologist
inventor, investigator	racecar driver, reporter	

See page 12 for a different booklet option.

Dressed to a T!

These bears build letter-sound associations too! Instead of decorating a beginning letter bear as described in Steps 4 and 5 on page 11, make a copy of the T-shirt pattern below. Have the student draw on the T-shirt an object that begins with the matching letter's sound; then help her cut out the pattern and glue it to the bear.

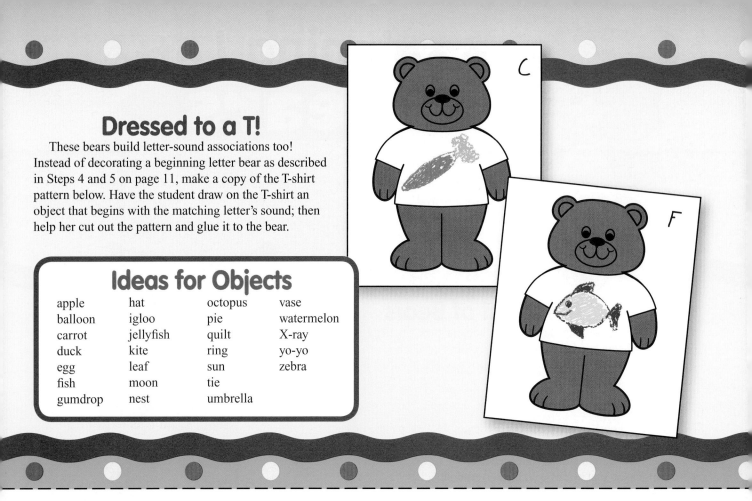

Ideas for Objects

apple	hat	octopus	vase
balloon	igloo	pie	watermelon
carrot	jellyfish	quilt	X-ray
duck	kite	ring	yo-yo
egg	leaf	sun	zebra
fish	moon	tie	
gumdrop	nest	umbrella	

T-shirt Pattern
Use with "Dressed to a T" on this page.

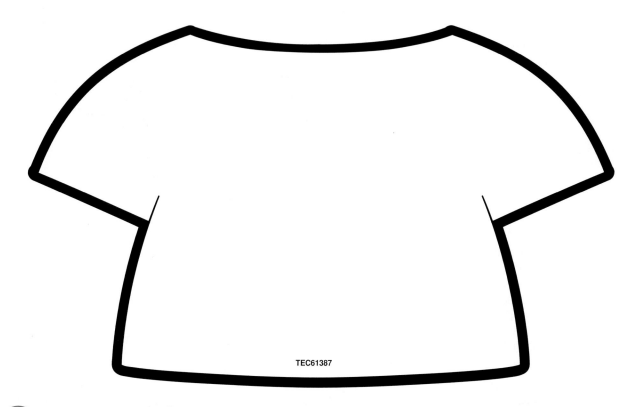

TEC61387

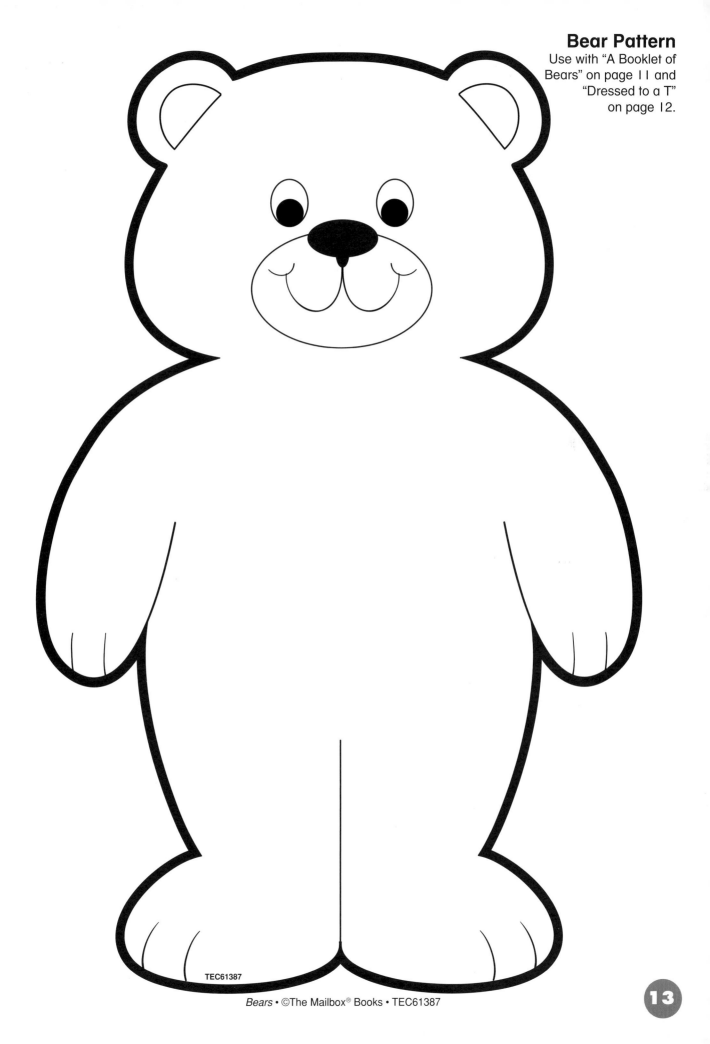

Bear Pattern
Use with "A Booklet of
Bears" on page 11 and
"Dressed to a T"
on page 12.

TEC61387

Bear Snores On

Written by Karma Wilson
Illustrated by Jane Chapman

While Bear takes his winter nap, forest animals take shelter in his nice warm cave. Their impromptu party eventually wakes Bear, but instead of being angry with his uninvited guests, he just wants to be included in the fun!

ideas contributed by Lynn Wagoner, Greensboro, NC

Rhyme Time

Developing rhyming skills

Little ones are sure to enjoy this interactive rereading of the story! As you read the story aloud, pause before each rhyming word and then prompt youngsters to supply the word. Also encourage students to add sound effects to the rereading by having them snore loudly each time you read the words "But the bear snores on." What fun!

Pretend Bears, Real Bears

Distinguishing real from pretend

Bear cries, talks, and drinks tea! Help young-sters sort these pretend bear behaviors from real bear behaviors. In advance, draw two simple caves on a sheet of chart paper and label the caves as shown. Then program paper strips naming real bear behaviors and the pretend behaviors of the bear in the book. After a read-aloud of the story, have students help you sort the strips onto the caves.

Real Bear

Bears have babies called cubs.
Bears can be dangerous.
Bears eat berries and fish.

Pretend Bear

Bear snores.
Bear cries.
Bear drinks tea.
Bear talks.

Aaaa-choooo!

The bear sneezes and wakes up.
The bear is happy.

Pepper Project

Dictating, retelling a story

At the end of the story, a small fleck of pepper causes Bear to sneeze and wake up. Help youngsters retell the story up to the appearance of the pepper. Then have each child dictate about the ending with this adorable project! To make the project, a child colors and cuts out a copy of the pot pattern on page 15. Then he glues the pot to a sheet of construction paper programmed as shown. He brushes glue above the pot and sprin-kles black hole-punched dots (pepper) over the glue. Then he dictates a sentence or two to describe the end of the story.

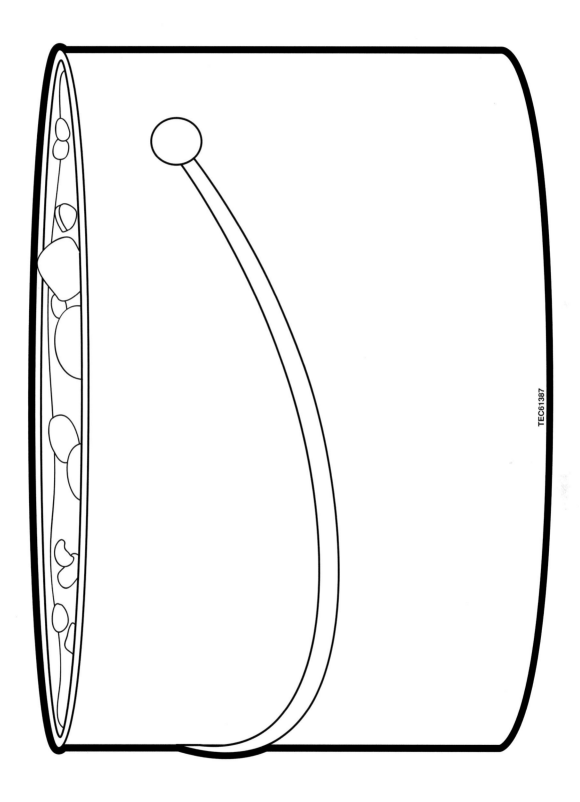

TEC61387

The "Bear-y" Best of Frank Asch

In Frank Asch's popular Bear series, brief text and simple illustrations portray a naive bear's grin-inducing adventures. Use the learning activities that follow with two of the books. Your students are sure to chuckle at Bear's misconceptions!

ideas by Julie Hays
Foothills Elementary, Maryville, TN

Happy Birthday, Moon
by Frank Asch
One day Bear decides to give the moon a birthday present. When Bear talks to the moon to find out what it would like, he doesn't realize that the responses he hears are his own echoes!

What better prop for this story recall activity than a hat? After all, Bear thinks a hat is a fitting gift for both the moon and himself! To prepare, trim about two inches from the opening of a brown paper lunch bag. Then glue a construction paper top hat to the bag as shown. Cut out a copy of the picture cards on page 17. Place the cards in the hat.

After reading the book aloud, present the hat to students with great fanfare and suggest that it is Bear's missing hat. Wonder aloud what is inside the hat. Then ask a child to remove a card from it and show it to his classmates. Ask the youngster to identify the picture and tell how it relates to the story. Invite his classmates to add to his comments. Then collect the card and have a different student remove another card. Continue in this manner until all of the cards have been discussed. ***Recalling story details***

Bear Shadow
by Frank Asch
After Bear's shadow scares away the fish he wants to catch, he tries to get rid of the shadow in a variety of entertaining ways.

No doubt Bear would enjoy reeling in a big catch with this comprehension follow-up! Program each of several construction paper fish (pattern on page 17) with a different one of the following words: *how, what, why.* Attach a paper clip to each fish and then put the fish in a pail. To make a fishing pole, attach a length of string to one end of an unsharpened pencil and then tie a magnet to the free end of the string.

To begin, invite a child to catch a fish with the fishing pole. Then use the word in a story-related question (see the examples). After students answer the question, have a different student hook a fish. Continue in this manner for a desired number of questions, returning the fish to the pail as needed. ***Answering comprehension questions***

Why does Bear want to get rid of his shadow?
How does Bear try to make his shadow go away?
What do you think Bear should know about shadows?
What part of the story do you like the most?

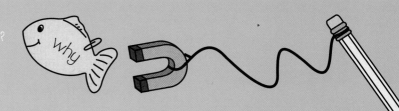

tree

river

forest

mountains

piggy bank

hat

wind

doorstep

Fish Pattern
Use with *"Bear Shadow"* on page 16.

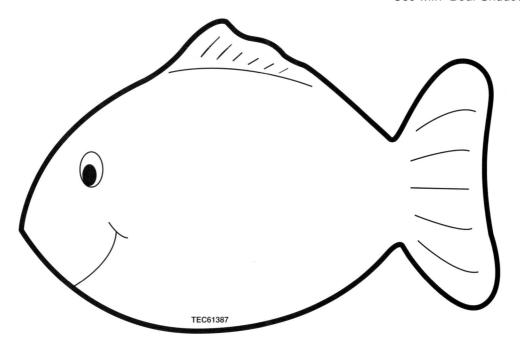

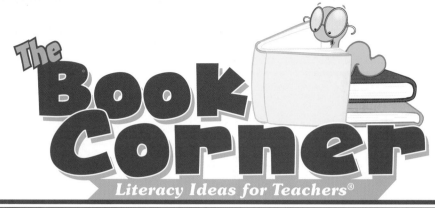

The Book Corner

Literacy Ideas for Teachers®

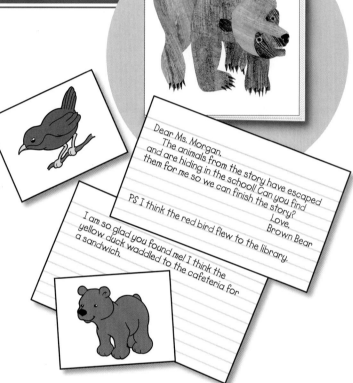

Bill Martin Jr / Eric Carle

Brown Bear, Brown Bear, What Do You See?

Brown Bear, Brown Bear, What Do You See?

Written by Bill Martin Jr.
Illustrated by Eric Carle
A series of colorful sightings begins when Brown Bear spies a bird in this rhythmic and classic read-aloud.

When youngsters are familiar with this story, take them on a scavenger hunt to find all the colorful critter characters! Make a copy of the cards on page 19. Place the card showing the bear in your classroom, along with a letter similar to the one shown. Then place the remaining cards in different locations throughout your school, leaving a hint with each card to lead youngsters to the next location. To begin, read the letter from Brown Bear. Then guide youngsters to the next location and help them find the card and hint. Continue until all the story characters have been found. *Following directions*

Lori Morgan, Woodrow Wilson Elementary, Hays, KS

Dear Ms. Morgan,
The animals from the story have escaped and are hiding in the school! Can you find them for me so we can finish the story?
Love,
Brown Bear
PS I think the red bird flew to the library.

I am so glad you found me! I think the yellow duck waddled to the cafeteria for a sandwich.

Corduroy

By Don Freeman
Corduroy, a toy bear in a store, goes on a search for his lost button. He is eventually found by the night watchman and taken back to the toy section where he belongs. The next morning, Corduroy is bought by Lisa, who takes him home and gives him a new button.

Give each child a colorful copy of page 20 and have her dictate for you to write her favorite part of the story on the overalls. Next, have her attach a craft foam circle (button) to the overalls. If desired, display the overalls with a bear cutout and the title "We Love Corduroy 'Overall' Other Bears!" *Making connections*

adapted from an idea by Felice Kestenbaum
Goosehill Primary School
Cold Spring Harbor, NY

I like when Corduroy tries to get the button off the mattress. It is funny.

Use with *"Brown Bear, Brown Bear, What Do You See?"* on page 18.

TEC61387

Note to the teacher: Use with *"Corduroy"* on page 18.

Storytime

A Splendid Friend, Indeed
Written and illustrated by Suzanne Bloom

A talkative goose likes doing all the things Bear is doing—so much so that it takes over all of Bear's activities, leading Bear to feel quite annoyed! Then Goose does something touching, sparking an unlikely friendship between the pair.

ideas contributed by Elizabeth Cook
St. Louis, MO

Yes, because they are reading together!

Before You Read
Display the cover of the book and have students describe what they see. Direct their attention to how the animals are sitting and the way they are looking at each other. Then say, "Bear and Goose are very different. Do you think they can be friends?" After youngsters share their thoughts, have them settle in for this entertaining read with a very special ending.

I have a friend named <u>Carly</u>. We are different because...

she likes to swing and I like to go down the slide.

Kristy

After You Read
Elicit a discussion about friendship, leading youngsters to understand that people can be friends whether they are alike or different. Next, give each child a paper programmed as shown. Encourage her to dictate to complete the prompt. Then have her illustrate her words. If desired, bind the pages between two covers with the title "We Are Friends: Alike or Different!"

B Is for Bear

Identifying letter sounds

Cute bears help bind these simple *b* booklets. To prepare, cut out a tagboard copy of the bear pattern on page 33 for each child. Have each youngster color her bear. Use hot glue to attach a clothespin to the back of each child's cutout. Provide each student with several half sheets of paper and a discarded magazine. Instruct her to tear or cut out pictures of items that begin with the /b/ sound and glue them to the booklet pages. Help her write a *b* next to each picture. Then help her to stack the pages and use her bear clip to secure the pages.

adapted from an idea by Dawn Schollenberger—Gr. K
Mary S. Shoemaker School, Woodstown, NJ

Animal Sightings

Word recognition, sentence formation

Count on this "bear-y" simple idea to strengthen a range of literacy skills. In advance, attach a bear cutout to one end of a pointer. Share with students Bill Martin Jr.'s *Brown Bear, Brown Bear, What Do You See?* Then display in a pocket chart the first sentence shown. Next, invite students to name various animals and their colors. Use students' suggestions and the format shown to prepare sentences for the amounts one through four or more. Then add the last sentence to the pocket chart. Read the sentences with students, using the pointer to direct attention to each word. After students are familiar with the sentences, choose from the ideas below to reinforce selected skills.

> Brown bear, brown bear, what do you see?
>
> I see one red fox.
>
> I see two yellow chicks.
>
> I see three green frogs.
>
> I see four white rabbits.
>
> I see a lot of animals looking at me!

- **Recognizing words:** On each sentence strip, add a visual clue for each number, color, or animal word. Name several of the words and have volunteers point them out.

- **Matching words:** Prepare separate word cards (with or without visual clues) for the number, color, and animal words. Have volunteers place each card atop the matching word in the pocket chart.

Ideas • • • • • • • •

"Paws" for Names
Phonological awareness

When it comes to helping students feel like part of the class, this idea is right on track! For each student, label a three-inch square and a white pawprint pattern (page 34) with his name. Within student reach, post the squares along a wall to resemble a trail. Instruct each youngster to lightly color his pawprint. Then have him find his name and tape his print atop the square. After the trail of prints is complete, invite students to sit near the display. Ask a student to point out his name and read it aloud. Then, as you repeat his name with students, lead them in clapping the number of parts (syllables). Highlight each youngster's name in this way.

Lynn C. Mode, Benton Heights Elementary, Monroe, NC

Bear Pair
Rhyming

Count on plenty of smiles and improved rhyming skills with this puppet idea. For each youngster, cut out a brown construction paper copy of the puppet pattern (page 35) along the outer edges. Fold the pattern in half; then trim the paper between the ears. Tape a craft stick inside and glue the pattern closed.

To begin, ask each student to hold her puppet. Announce the word *bear* and one other word. If the words rhyme, each student shows you the smiling side of her puppet. If they do not rhyme, she displays the frowning side. Scan students' puppets and confirm the correct response. Then continue with a desired number of rhyming and nonrhyming word pairs, including the word *bear* in each pairing.

Lynn C. Mode

Paw Path

Counting

Make a gameboard similar to the one shown. (Hint: a pawprint stamp is a handy tool for making the path!) Two youngsters each place a bear manipulative on the path. In turn, each student rolls the die and counts aloud the dots on top. Then he moves his bear the corresponding number of pawprints. Play continues in the same manner until each bear reaches the cave.

adapted from an idea by Amy Durrwachter
Kirkwood Early Childhood Center, Kirkwood, MO

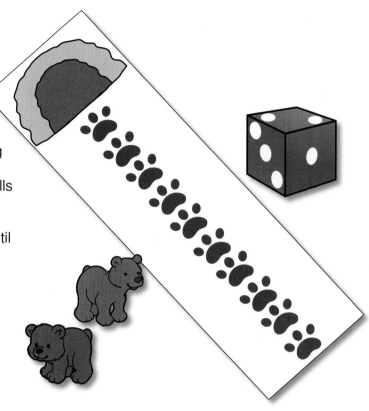

Bears in a Cave

Comparing sets

Give each child in a small group a cave cutout and ten bear-shaped crackers. Also give each child a card that shows a number from 1 to 10. Ask each child to read his card and put the matching number of bears on his cave. To guide youngsters to compare their bear sets, ask, "Which cave has the most (fewest) bears?" Continue by collecting the cards and repeating the activity. Then invite little ones to eat their bears.

Leslie Blom, Central Elementary, Bellevue, NE

Bear Families
Sorting
To prepare, fill a small bowl with bear-shaped cookies in two different colors. Set out two construction paper copies of the cottage on page 36; then place a different-colored bear on each cottage door. A youngster visits the center and sorts the bears into their matching families. When he is finished, he nibbles on a separate cup of bear cookies set aside for a snack.

Jennifer Gemar, Tripp-Delmont Schools, Tripp, SD

Who Has Your Fish?
Participating in a group activity
To prepare for this circle-time activity, make a fish cutout from tagboard. Invite a child to pretend to be a grizzly bear and have him sit with his back to the class. Give the fish to one of the students and have him conceal the fish by sitting on it. Then encourage youngsters to chant, "Grizzly bear, grizzly bear, who has your fish?" Encourage the grizzly bear to turn around and guess who has his fish, prompting him to use his classmates' names and allowing him several guesses. When the fish is found, have the child who was hiding the fish become the new grizzly bear!

Suzanne Moore, Irving, TX

Bear Booklet
Dictating information

This booklet-making project is the perfect complement to Bill Martin Jr.'s book *Brown Bear, Brown Bear, What Do You See?* After reading aloud the book, explain that authors often use their five senses to imagine what it would be like to be a character in a book. Next, share some basic facts about brown bears. Then ask each child to imagine that he is a brown bear. Use the directions below to help each child make a bear booklet. Have him complete the sentence on each booklet page by drawing or dictating a response.

Steps to make one bear booklet:
1. Make a cover by decorating a brown seven-inch paper oval to look like a bear head. If desired, cut ears from construction paper scraps and glue them to the head.
2. Cut six seven-inch ovals (booklet pages) from blank paper.
3. Glue each sentence strip from a copy of the bottom of page 33 to a separate booklet page.
4. Staple the pages in order behind the cover.

Laurie K. Gibbons, Huntsville, AL

Good Eats!
Identifying needs of a living thing

Help youngsters recognize common foods in a bear's diet with this toe-tapping song and activity! Give each youngster a copy of page 37. Have children point to the bear. Explain that many bears eat a variety of things they can find in or near a forest, such as fish, berries, acorns, and honey. Instruct each child to point to each of these food items pictured on the page. Then lead students in singing the song, encouraging them to point to each type of food when appropriate. If desired, have each child color his page before taking it home to show to his family.

(sung to the tune of "My Bonnie Lies Over the Ocean")

Some bears eat the fish in the river.
Some bears like the berries so sweet.
Some bears eat the nuts from the forest.
Some bears think that honey's a treat.
Yummy honey, some bears think that honey's a special treat!
Yummy honey, and that's what some bears like to eat!

Suzanne Moore, Irving, TX

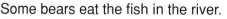

"Beary" Simple

Art

Whether you use this idea to complement a favorite bear book or to reinforce the letter *B*, it's sure to prompt lots of smiles! To make one bear, stuff a medium brown paper lunch bag with newspaper. Fold over the top two inches of the bag and then staple the bag closed. Next, cut out a brown bear head, two brown arms, and two brown feet (patterns on page 38). Draw a face on the bear. Cut two inner ears from pink construction paper and glue them in place. Glue the head to the top of the bag. Glue the arms to the back of the bag and the feet to the bottom of the bag as shown. Cut two small ovals from black construction paper and glue them to the paws. Draw details on the feet as shown. Finally, glue a 3½" x 5" brown oval to the bear's belly.

Dick Freeman, Benson Hill Elementary, Renton, WA

A "Bear-y" Special Message

Art

Here's a card that's just perfect for any occasion! To make one, cut out a large brown paper bear like the one shown. Glue paper shapes to the bear to make paws, ears, and a face; then draw details. Next, cut out a copy of the poem on page 39 and glue it to the bear. When the glue is dry, sign the card and fold the bear's arms to conceal the poem.

Diane White
Burlington Parks and Recreation Department
   Preschool
Burlington, Ontario, Canada

You Are "Bear-y" Special!

Roses are red.
Violets are blue.
This little bear
Has a big hug for you!

Sweet Dreams

Song

How do bears adapt to winter? That's what students learn with this song! After students are familiar with the lyrics, explain that some scientists do not consider bears true hibernators. Tell students that bears sometimes wake during mild weather. Follow up with a variation of the song, changing the first three lines to "Sometimes bears wake when it's warm out" and the fourth line to "To stretch and eat some food." Modify the rest of the song to say that if it's not spring, the bears go back to sleep!

Deborah Gibbone, St. Andrew the Apostle School, Drexel Hill, PA

(sung to the tune of "The Bear Went Over the Mountain")

Bears sleep a lot in the winter.
Bears sleep a lot in the winter.
Bears sleep a lot in the winter.
So they stay safe and warm.

So they stay safe and warm.
So they stay safe and warm.
[They grow their fur long and shaggy.]
[They grow their fur long and shaggy.]
[They grow their fur long and shaggy.]
So they stay safe and warm.

So they stay safe and warm.
So they stay safe and warm.
[They grow their fur long and shaggy.]
So they stay safe and warm.

Suggestions for additional verses:
They eat and eat to get fatter.
They find a safe, cozy shelter.

Down by the Bear Cave

Song

Your little cubs will pretend to fill up on tasty bear treats while singing this song. Sing the verses below, substituting other bear foods, such as termites and berries, in the second verse. A growlin' good breakfast!

(sung to the tune of "Down by the Station")

Down by the bear cave early in the morning,
See the little bear cubs all in a row.
See the mama bear; she's bringing home some honey.
Yum, yum! Chomp, chomp!
Down it goes!

Down by the bear cave early in the morning,
See the little bear cubs all in a row.
See the mama bear; she's bringing home some [fishies].
Yum, yum! Chomp, chomp!
Down they go!

Daphne L. Rivera—Gr. K, Bob Sikes Elementary School, Crestview, FL

A "Bear-y" Good Year!

Classroom Decorations

- Display on the classroom door an enlarged bear cutout (pattern on page 40) and the title "A 'Bear-y' Merry Welcome." Around the bear post bear paw cutouts (patterns on page 40) programmed with student names.
- Use brown bulletin board paper to make a bear cave in your reading area. Provide teddy bears for students to read to at the cave.

Classroom Labels

- Label a bear paw cutout (patterns on page 40) for each student. Use the paws to label student cubbies or desks.
- Label an index card for each classroom area or center. At each area, place a teddy bear holding the label.
- To make a job chart, label paper cave shapes with jobs. Label bear cutouts (pattern on page 40) with student names. To assign jobs, attach a bear to each cave.

Ada Goren, Winston-Salem, NC

Shhh! These bears are sleeping! Display some of your students' best bear artwork in a snowy cave. Crumple brown craft paper and attach it to a bulletin board to make a cave shape. Add some white cotton batting around and on top of the cave for snow. Then mount student-made bears inside the cave and add a title.

Bonnie Martin, Hopewell Country Day School, Pennington, NJ

Brown Bear, Brown Bear, What Do You See in the Winter?

an orange scarf

a purple present

a white snowflake

black boots

red mittens

a silver shovel

No doubt your students know and love *Brown Bear, Brown Bear, What Do You See?* by Bill Martin Jr., so they're sure to enjoy this approach to exploring seasonal sights. Post the title shown and a bear. Cut several wintertime items from white paper. Have students embellish each item with a different color of arts-and-crafts materials. Then display the items with labels similar to the ones shown.

Heather Taylor, Melville, NY

Shhhh! Sleeping Bear

I think bears dreem about food. Thay lik to eat.

Long Winter's Nap

This display is an adorable reminder that some animals sleep a lot during this time of year. Bring in a toy stuffed bear and suggest to students that it needs a cozy place to sleep. With students' help, decorate a large cardboard box with brown paper and cotton (snow) so that it resembles a cave. Post a sleeping bear sign similar to the one shown. Then have each youngster dictate what bears might dream about. Place students' papers and the bear in the cave. When spring arrives, have each youngster dictate to tell the bear about the change in seasons. Then welcome the bear from the cave!

Erica Cerwin, Bob Beard Elementary, Helotes, TX

KIDS IN THE KITCHEN

Little ones will delight in arranging bears around their own edible campfires with this snack!

To prepare for the snack:

- Collect the necessary ingredients and utensils using the lists on the recipe card below.
- Photocopy the step-by-step recipe cards on page 32.
- Cut out the cards and display them in the snack area.
- Follow the teacher preparation guidelines for the snack.

Camping Bears

Ingredients for one:
pretzel sticks
Teddy Grahams graham snacks
orange spray cheese

Utensils and supplies:
disposable plate for each child

Teacher preparation:
Arrange the ingredients and supplies near the step-by-step recipe cards.

Janet Boyce
Cokato, MN

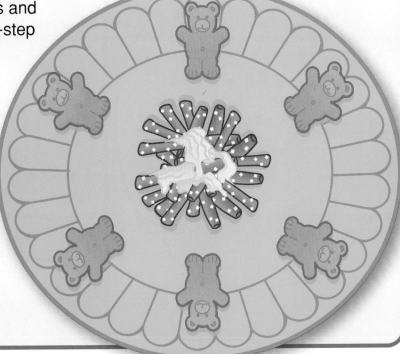

Recipe Cards

Use with "Camping Bears" on page 31.

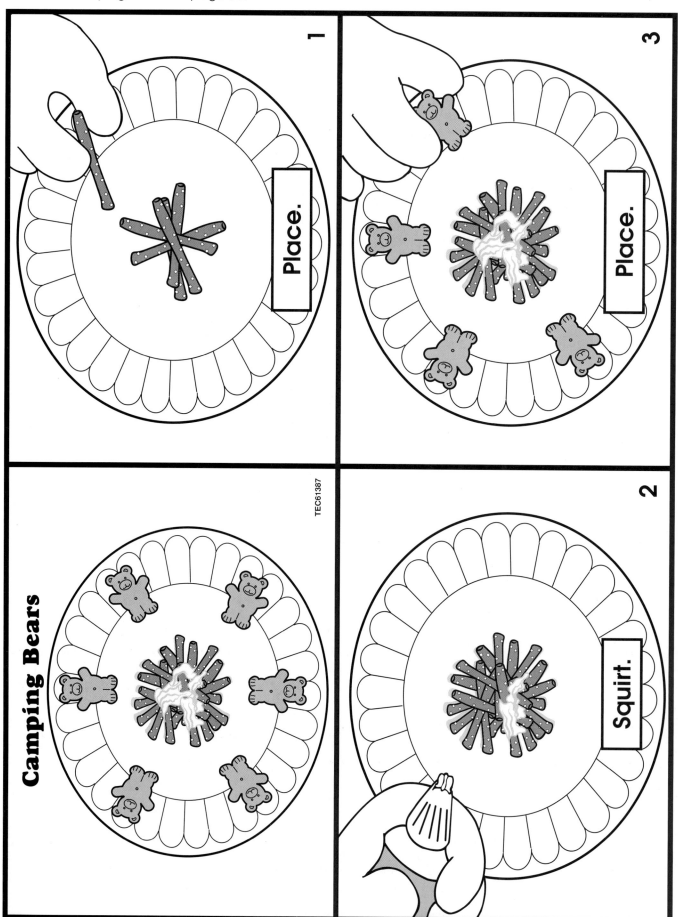

Sentence Strips
Use with "Bear Booklet" on page 26.

1 If I were a bear,	2 I would see
3 I would smell	4 I would hear
5 I would feel	6 I would taste

Pawprint Pattern
Use with "'Paws' for Names" on page 23.

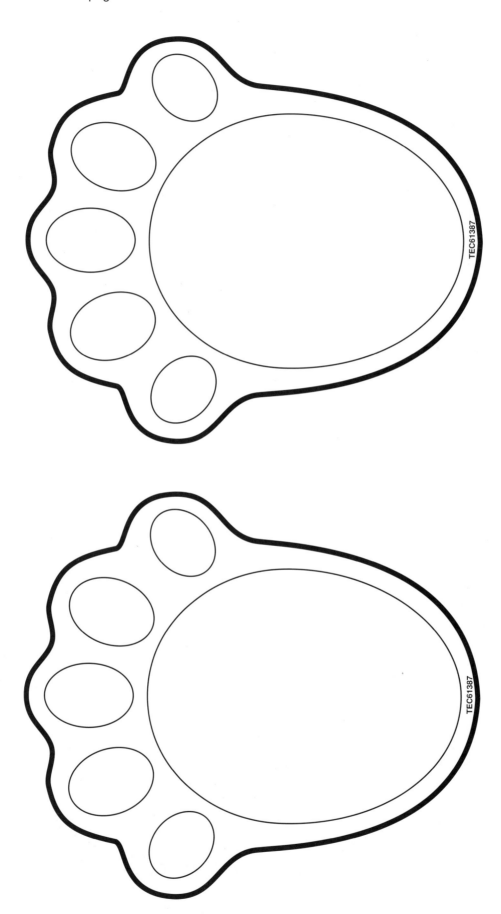

TEC61387

TEC61387

TEC61387

Note to the teacher: Use with "Bear Families" on page 25.

Name

"Bear-y" Good Food

Listen for directions.

Bears • ©The Mailbox® Books • TEC61387

Note to the teacher: Use with "Good Eats!" on page 26.

Bear Patterns
Use with "'Beary' Simple" on page 27.

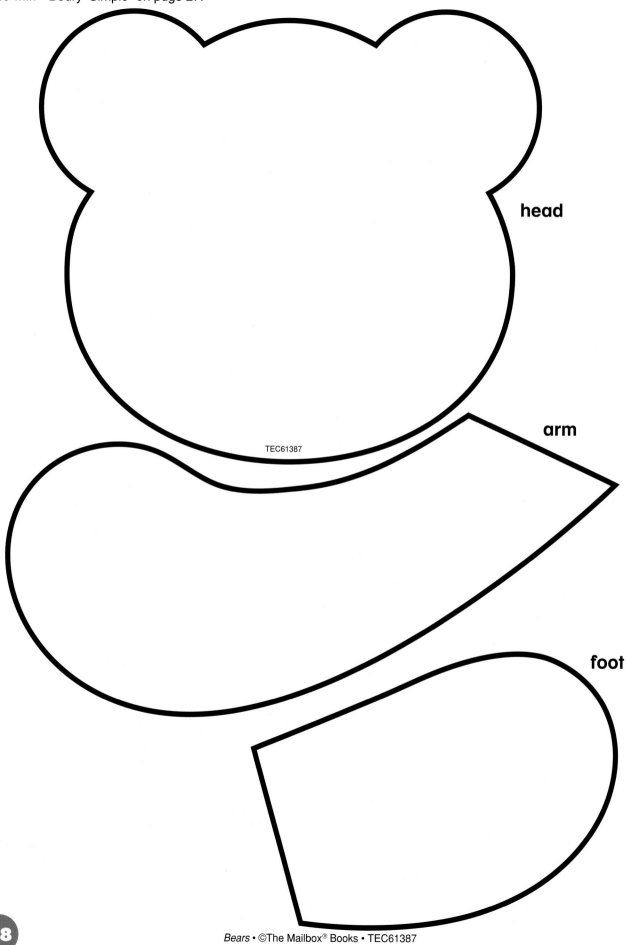

head

arm

foot

TEC61387

You Are "Bear-y" Special!

Roses are red.
Violets are blue.
This little bear
Has a big hug for you!

You Are "Bear-y" Special!

Roses are red.
Violets are blue.
This little bear
Has a big hug for you!

Bear and Paw Patterns
Use with "A 'Bear-y' Good Year!" on page 29.

TEC61387

TEC61387

TEC61387

"I Am 'Bear-y' Special" Booklet

How to Use Pages 42 and 43

Use this booklet to record your youngsters' name-writing and drawing skills. Give each child a copy of pages 42 and 43. Read the text on each booklet page to students. Then help each child follow the directions below to make a booklet.

Directions for Each Student

1. Draw a picture of you on the booklet cover. Write your name.
2. Draw yourself doing something you are good at on booklet page 1.
3. Draw and color your favorite food on booklet page 2.
4. Draw and color your favorite toy on booklet page 3.
5. Cut out the booklet pages, sequence them, and staple them together along the left-hand side.

Finished Sample

I Am "Bear-y" Special

by_____

I am good at...

1

My favorite food is...

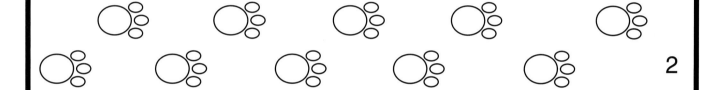

2

My favorite toy is...

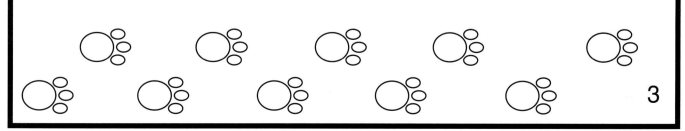

3

Name

44

Building Blocks

Circle the blocks that are the **same**.

Cross off the blocks that are **different**.

Name _____

Cute as a Button

🖍 Color by the code.

Color Code

◯ — red

▢ — blue

Name _____

Bear Essentials

 Trace.  Cut.

 Count.

 Glue to match.

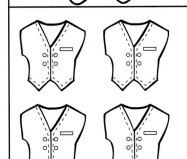

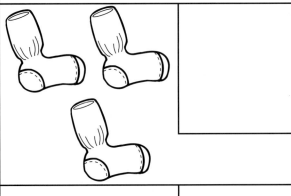

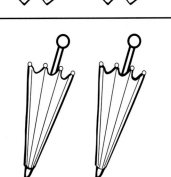

1   5   4   3   2

Name _____

Favorite Fruit Pies

What comes next?

✂ Cut. 🖊 Glue.

Name _____

Balancing Bear

Color the rhyming pictures the same color on each ball.

Bears • ©The Mailbox® Books • TEC61387